PAGES and LEAFLETS of NORTH OXFORDSHIRE

My Lineage Pre-1700–1959

A FAMILY AND RELIGIOUS HISTORY

Angela Fortnum

authorHOUSE®

AuthorHouse™ UK
1663 Liberty Drive
Bloomington, IN 47403 USA
www.authorhouse.co.uk
Phone: 0800.197.4150

Published by AuthorHouse   09/20/2018

ISBN: 978-1-5462-9795-6 (sc)
ISBN: 978-1-5462-9796-3 (hc)
ISBN: 978-1-5462-9794-9 (e)

Print information available on the last page.

This book is printed on acid-free paper.

Contents

"A well-researched and written book by a new author that will be of interest to family historians. Sociologists, anthropologists together with religious historians could also find aspects of interest.

The book tells the story of eight generations of her maternal grandfathers. Not only are there some interesting details of the progression from agricultural labourer to self-employed and then small holders but also, the changes in religious beliefs over time.

At the end of the book she has brought the family line up-to-date by including details of the last two generations namely, her mother and herself.

The richness and diversity of the Church and Chapel buildings that were linked in some way to the family tell a story of their own in respect of the local history."

In remembrance of my mother, Muriel Page, who inspired me to research my roots. She often regaled me with tales of life at South Newington Mill and about my great-grandfather Charles when he was getting older and lived at Wigginton.

Acknowledgements

Thank you to relatives who provided information and to the staff of Banbury Library for their help and patience in answering many questions.

Also, to Katrina Paynton-Gilkes, who acted as my sounding board.

Special thanks go to Brian Curtis for graciously consenting to the use of his church photographs and for providing unadulterated copies.

Last, but not least, I am grateful for the help and guidance given to me by Dorothy Lee, Coleen Medina, and the team at Author House.

Introduction

My mother, Muriel Page, was born at South Newington Mill in 1916, and I became curious to learn about my roots and began to research my maternal grandparents. I succeeded in getting back to my seven-times-great-grandfather and found that my direct ancestors came from Milcombe and South Newington, two villages in north Oxfordshire, England.

As I progressed, I realised there was a story to tell, not only about the social history but also about the changing religious beliefs and the historic buildings linked to these, a book to appeal to people with differing interests.

For the guidance of the reader, leaving Bloxham, St Mary's on your left, take the first left at the roundabout to Barford St Michael. Otherwise, follow the A361. You will find the turn to Milcombe on your right. Back on the A361 continue to South Newington, which has several sharp, dangerous bends; this is the main road for heavy-goods vehicles. Take the left turn opposite the public house, which will take you to the entrance of St Peter's Church. From South Newington take the A361 to Wigginton, which is on the right.

Chapter 1

Possible Origin of Name

Perhaps the most obvious origin goes back to when people were named after their occupations, before William the Conqueror introduced hereditary surnames. The surname Page was derived from the Middle English and Old French *page*.

Spelling variations were commonplace due to the illiteracy of all but the wealthy. The main spellings were Page and Paige, although there are others, including Padge.

Chapter 2

James Page: Seven-Times-GGF

When researching the birth of my seven-times-GGF I only found one record for a James Page. He was baptised at Much Haddon on 28 November 1770 but, unfortunately, he died and was buried three days later.

This led me to believe James was possibly a Quaker. However, there is no paper trail from Quaker meetings to substantiate this theory except the burial details of his son James, born in 1702, who died as an infant. The parish record for St Peter ad Vincula records his burial on 22 February as:

PAGE James s. James and Dorathy of Milcomb [sic] bur. in Ye meeting yard.

A small group of Quakers formed by 1663, but the Friends meeting house, with adjoining land, was not constructed until 1693. It was closed and leased to the Methodists in 1825, although the Quakers occasionally continued to use the building. The property was bought by George Dyson, a local resident, and in 1928, it was given to the village and is still used as the village hall.

South Newington Village Hall, 2016, by Angela Fortnum.

James and Dorathy had six children: four boys and two girls. There is no trace in the parish records of South Newington or Milcombe, however, that any of them were baptised into the Church of England as children, although the three surviving sons all married in the church. The two girls were beneficiaries under the will of John Rymell of London (formerly of Great Tew, a village near South Newington). John was possibly a brother of Dorathy, as he refers to Mary and Elizabeth as his nieces.

As transcribed from a copy of the original document.
Original line- and page-breaks are not preserved.

In the name of God Amen I John Rymell Citizen and Joyner of
London being of sound and perfect mind and memory and good of
understanding thanks be to Almighty God for the same do hereby make
and ordain this my last Will and Testament in manner following
That is to say first and principally I recommend my soul into the hands
of Almighty God that gave it hoping for Eternal Life and for my body
I commit to the earth to be decently buried according to the discretion
of my Executor hereinafter named and for what of this worldly goods as
God in mercy hath lent me I dispose thereof as followeth
Imprimis I give and bequeath unto Elizabeth Katch Wife of John Katch
Citizen of London Coach Wheeler one shilling
Item I give and bequeath unto Elizabeth Lockton Daughter of Robert
Lockton twenty shillings
Item I give and bequeath unto the Daughters of William Smith of
Witney five shillings apiece
Item I give and bequeath unto Charles Rymell senior of Great Tew one
shilling
Item I give unto Elizabeth Page Daughter of James Page of Millcomb
the sum of ten pounds Then my will is that those my aforesaid Legacies
should be paid within two years next after my decease and also my will
is that my Executrix should cause to order a tombstone to be layed on
me as I have done in like manner for my Wife
Lastly I do hereby make and ordain my Niece Mary Page Daughter of
James Page of Millcomb full and sole Executrix of this my last Will and
Testament and also giving her the Middle Park during the life of the holder
with all the rest of my Goods and Chattels whatsoever as I may die possessed
of her and her heirs forever she paying all my just debts and Legacies and
funeral expenses and do hereby owe this to be my last Will and Testament
disannulling and making void all other Wills heretofore by me made
In Witness hereunto this Twenty Sixth Day of May One Thousand
Seven Hundred and Twenty Nine I do set my hand and seal

Signed sealed published and declared by the testator to be
His last Will and Testament in the presence of us
Henery Banond?   Marke
Robert Clifford   John Rymell
John Baggs

Probate granted 27th August 1730 to Mary Page

A true and perfect Inventory of all the singular of the Goods and Chattels and Chattels of John Rymell Citizen and Joyner of London late deceased and of late residence in Great Tew in the County of Oxon ___ And appraised by us William Caxton Henery Stowe John Baggs this 27 day of August in the year of our Lord 1730

		li – s – d
Imprimis	his wearing apparel	05 – 00 – 00
Item	the Clock	01 – 01 – 00
Item	two bedsteads and bedding thereunto	02 – 00 – 00
Item	a table 4 chairs boxes and other lumber	02 – 00 – 00
Item	brasse and Pewter	02 – 00 – 00
Item	In the Cellar tubbs and barrels and other lumber	01 – 00 – 00
Item	wood in the yard	00 – 05 – 00
Item	Money on Bond	50 – 00 – 00
	Total	63 – 06 – 00

William   Cockson
Henry   Stow
John Baggs

Chapter 3

John Page: Six-Times-GGF

John was one of four sons born to James Page and Dorathy of Milcombe. I assume the family were Quakers. Due to the lack of Friends meeting records, James's date of birth is not available. However, the parish register for 27 April 1727, St Mary's Parish Church, Banbury, Oxfordshire, records that he was baptised as an adult.

Later that year, on 26 September, he married Mary White.

John of Milcombe and Mary of South Newington, married by Mr Andrews, Vicar of South Newington (by Banns).

On 9 April 1767, John was buried in the churchyard of St Peter ad Vincula, Newington South. His wife predeceased him in 1764.

John and Mary had four children: one son, John (5×GGF), and three daughters. Sadly, one of the girls died in infancy and the others died as teenagers.

Mary Paige 1731–1733

Elizabeth (Betty) Paige 1733–1749

Mary Paige 1736–1749

The Parish Register of St Mary, Banbury:

16 November 1749. PAGE Elizabeth and Mary ds of John, weaver and Mary.

This information suggests they may have died due to an epidemic, such as typhus or scarlatina, both of which were rife during the mid-1700s. But there is no reference as to the cause of death in the register.

John's occupation was a weaver, and he probably made cloth on handlooms, as the flying shuttlecock was not developed until 1733. This sped up the process and almost doubled production. Weaving was a small cottage industry in many surrounding villages. John was probably an artisan of his day.

Chapter 4

John Page: Five-Times-GGF

As indicated, John was the only surviving child of John and Mary. He was baptised on 28 July 1728 in the parish of Newington South, Oxfordshire.

On 10 March 1753, he married Sarah Geden at St Peter ad Vincula, Newington South. Due to the high illiteracy, many people did not know how to spell their names, and Sarah's family was no exception. There were several variations, including Geadon and Geddon, but today the generally accepted spelling is Gaydon. Sarah was born in Wigginton, although at the time of her marriage, she resided at South Newington. Her family originated from Tysoe, Warwickshire, and I traced the family back to Richard (circa 1600), my nine-times-GGF.

John and Sarah had twelve children: six sons, including James, my four-times-GGF, and six daughters. Sarah died in 1800 and was buried at South Newington on 12 March. John died in 1807 and was buried 26 April. The record in the parish register indicated he was parish clerk, but no dates are given. This is quite a change of direction from his Quaker ancestors.

John signed his will on 8 April 1803 and added a codicil on 8 March 1807, probably on his deathbed.

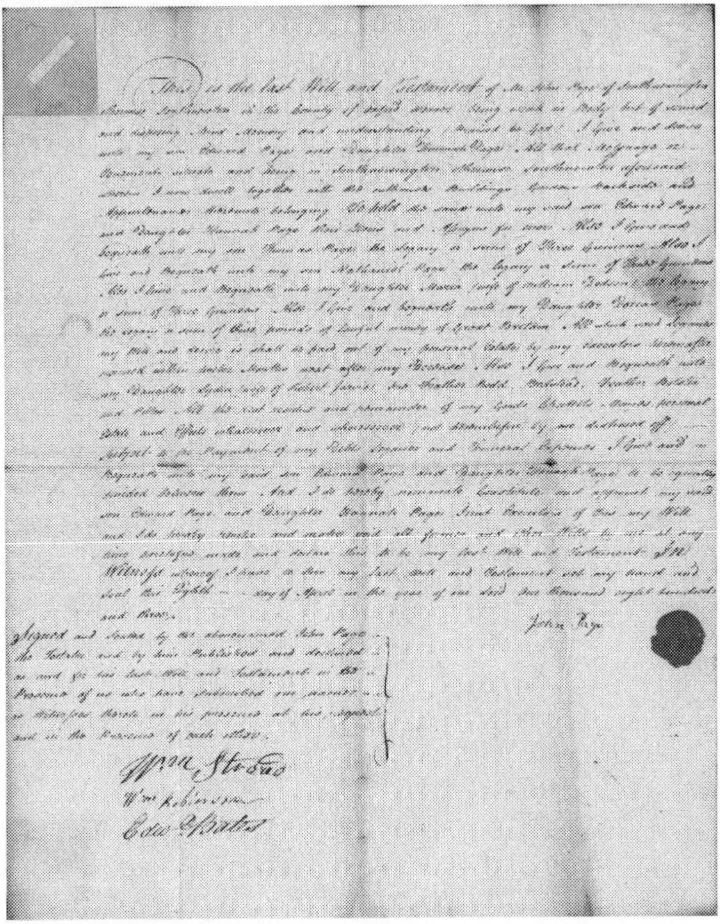

Findmypast.co.uk/oxfordshirewillsindex/1516-1857.

Transcription of will in clearer text. Lines and page breaks are not preserved. Spelling is as in the document.

This is the last Will and Testament of me John Page of Southnewington otherwise Southnewton in the County of Oxford weaver being weak in Body but of sound and disposing Mind Memory and uderstanding Praised be God I give and demise unto my son Edward Page and Daughter Hannah Page All that messuage or Tenement situate and being in Southnewington otherwise southnewton aforesaid wherein I now dwell together with the outhouse Buildings Garden Backside and appurtenances thereto belonging to hold the same unto my said son Edward Page and Daughter Hannah Page their heirs and assigns forever Also I Give and bequeath unto my son Thomas Page the Legacy or sum of Three Guineas Also I Give and Bequeath unto my son Nathaniel Page the legacy or sum of Three Guineas Also I give and Bequeath unto my daughter Maria wife of William Dodson the legacy or sum of Three Guineas Also I give and bequeath unto my Daughter Dorcas Page the legacy or sum of five pounds of lawful money of Great Britain all which said legacies my Will and desire is shall be paid out of my personal Estate by my Executors hereinafter named within twelve months next after my decease Also I give and bequeath unto my Daughter Lydia wife of Robert Jarvis one feather bed Bedstead Feather Bolster and Pillow All the rest residue of my Goods Chattels monies personal Estate and effects whatsoever and wheresoever not hereinbefore by me disposed off [sic] subject to the payment of my Debts Legacies and Funeral Expenses I give and Bequeath unto my said son Edward Page and my Daughter Hannah Page to be equally divided between them And I hereby do nominate and constitute and appoint my said son Edward Page and Daughter Hannah Page Joint Executors of this my Will and I do hereby revoke and make void all former and other Wills by me at any time herebefore made and declare this my last will and testament In Witness whereof I have set my hand seal this Eighth day of April in the year of our Lord One thousand eight hundred and three.

Signature of John Page SEAL

Signed and sealed by the abovementioned John Page the Testator and by him published and declared as and for his last Will and Testament in the presence of us who have subscribed our names as Witnesses thereto in his presence and in the presence of each other

Signed   Wm Stroud Wm Robinson Edward Bates

A codicil dated 8 March 1807 was added, but some of the detail differs from the will above, which would suggest the paper trail is incomplete. The document was witnessed by Harry Davis, Clerk, Robert Jarvis, and Lydia Jarvis.

Findmypast.co.uk/oxfordshirewillsindex/1516-1857

Transcription of codicil in clearer text. Lines and page breaks are not preserved. Spelling is as in the document.

South Newington March 8, 1807

Whereas I John Page of the Parish above mentioned did in my last will & Testament give a certain cottage to my Grandson John Page and there described and did direct him by my said Will to pay Ten Pounds to my Executors therein named now I do by this codicil to my said will revoke that part of my will and I do hereby bequeath the said House with its appurtenances to my Son Edward Page and my Daughter Hannah Page my aforesaid Executors and my further will is that they my aforesaid Executors should pay to my ~~Son~~ Grandson John son of James Page the sum of Ten Pounds to be paid within twelve calendar months after my decease and I desire that this may be considered and taken as a Codicil to my said will accordingly

Signed and sealed by me the testator as a Codicil to my last will the day and year above written   Signature of John Page   SEAL

The will with codicil was proved at Oxford on 20 May 1807 by oaths of Edward Page and Hannah Page. Death duty, amount not known, was paid at Oxford on 20 June 1807.

John and Sarah's grandson William, son of Nathaniel, was one of the first family members to emigrate to Canada. His first wife, Maria French, with whom he had eleven children, died, and he married Jane Elizabeth Tunks in 1858. He died in Elgin, Ontario. Descendants of William Page and Maria still live in Canada. Their family is the subject of my next book.

In the meanwhile, William and Maria's son Thomas married Sarah Herbert and their daughter Mary Anne married a distant cousin, John Tims Page, a son of Joseph Page (my two-times-GGF) and his wife Harriet. John was a baker and a Wesleyan Methodist. Both John and Mary Anne were buried in the Methodist section of Bloxham churchyard.

Bloxham is one of the larger villages in the area with cottages built of the local ironstone. Behind the high street are narrow lanes lined with this type of cottage.

A small building right of the church, was built in 1689 and is now the Bloxham Village Museum, which is open from Easter to October.

Chapter 5

James Page: Four-Times-GGF

James was the eldest son of John Page and Sarah Geden. He was born in 1753 at South Newington and baptised in the local parish church:

<u>1753</u> Dec 16   PAGE James s John and Sarah.

James married Sarah Pargeter at St Mary's Church, Bloxham, prior to which banns were read at South Newington:

<u>1775</u> PAGE James otp weaver. PARGETER Sarah Psh Bloxham. 28 May 4/11 June.

James's occupation suggests weaving was still a thriving industry.

<u>1775</u> Jul 10   PAGE James Psh South Newington xPARGETER Sarah otp Banns Wit. Thomas ROOKES John DAVIS

x denotes that Sarah made her mark as she was unable to sign her name.

John and Sarah had two sons: John, my four-times-GGF; and Joseph.

James died at Thorpe Mandeville, Northamptonshire, and was buried at Bloxham on 13 April 1823.

St Mary's Church, Bloxham

Photo: Brian Curtis

The church has a magnificent Gothic-style spire. The twelfth-century doorway was reset in the north wall, and there is fourteenth-century tracery throughout although, there are still some parts dating back to the twelfth century. There are too many features to cover here, but if in the area, I would recommend a visit.

Chapter 6

John Page: Three-Times-GGF

John was the elder of two sons born to James and Sarah Page. He was baptised at St Michael's Church Barford, St Michael.

<u>1776</u> Sep 22 PAGE John s James and Sarah (Bishop's Transcript PAIGE)

St Michael's Church, Barford St Michael

Photo: Brian Curtis

A very clean and well-looked-after Grade I listed twelfth-century church that is just beyond the village green. The bell tower, north doorway, and font are Norman, but most of the remainder was rebuilt in the early English style in the thirteenth century.

Barford St Michael, a twin village with Barford St John, separated by the River Swere, is the larger of the two villages. The houses and cottages are built in the local dark-honey-coloured stone, and many of the later developments are built to match the older properties.

John married twice: his first marriage was to Mary Cleaver and took place at South Newington Church:

1803 PAGE John otp. bch xCLEAVER Mary spinster Hamlet of Milcombe Psh of Bloxham by Banns. Wit.John BULL John PAGE.

x denotes that Mary made her mark as she was unable to sign her name.

John and Mary had five children, two girls and three boys, but sadly the eldest and youngest both died in infancy.

Alis (Alice) Page Baptised 29 January and Buried 9 February 1804. Alis was baptised in a private ceremony with her twin Sarah.

Henry Page baptised 29 April and buried 16 September 1810.

Their mother, Mary died in 1811 and was buried on12 July.

John was left with three young children and married his second wife, Hannah Braggins, at South Newington:

<u>1812</u> Jul 16 PAGE John wid. xBRAGGINS Hannah, spin, botp. By BANNS. Wit. William Scaysbrook and Elizabeth Scaysbrook.

Hannah was unable to sign her name and marked the register with an x

John and Hannah had five children: three sons, including my two-times-GGF Joseph, and two girls.

Circa 1819, John became parish clerk of South Newington Church, St Peter Ad Vincula, and retained this position until 1849. He was the second witness to many marriages in the church.

The 1841 census records John as a plush weaver living with his wife, Hannah, and three children: John, a tailor who remained single; Thomas; and Elizabeth.

Plush Weaving

The development of the loom meant that softer, finer plush fabrics were woven. Plush is a textile having a cut nap or pile with a feel of softness; originally, the pile of plush was of mohair or worsted. Weaving was a literal cottage industry. Often, the loom was upstairs, with the living quarters downstairs.

1841 Census for South Newington

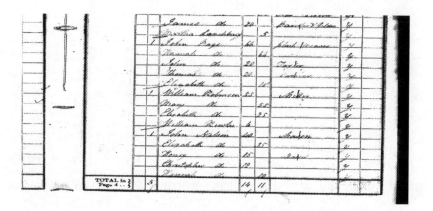

John died on 25 May1849 at South Newington and was buried in the churchyard of St Peter ad Vincula, South Newington:

<u>1849</u> May 28 PAGE John SN 73years Parish Clerk

Death Certificate, John Page 1849

CERTIFIED COPY OF AN ENTRY OF DEATH

GIVEN AT THE GENERAL REGISTER OFFICE

Application Number 9201488-1

REGISTRATION DISTRICT   BANBURY UNION

1849 DEATH in the Sub-district of Bloxham   in the   County of Oxford

No.	When and where died	Name and surname	Sex	Age	Occupation	Cause of death	Signature, description and residence of informant	When registered	Signature of registrar
906	Twenty fifth May 1849 North Newington	John Page	Male	78 years	Plush Weaver & Parish Clerk	Consumption not certified	William Gilo In Attendance South Newington	Second June 1849	John Bennet Registrar

CERTIFIED to be a true copy of an entry in the certified copy of a Register of Deaths in the District above mentioned.

Given at the GENERAL REGISTER OFFICE, under the Seal of the said Office, the   16th   day of   May   2018

DYE 266666

See note overleaf

1851 Census for South Newington

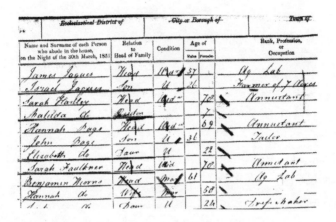

Hannah is an annuitant and is therefore in receipt of a pension or payment that protects income.

Hannah passed away on 22 August 1853 and was also buried at South Newington:

<u>1853</u> PAGE Hannah 72 years SN.

St Peter ad Vincula Parish Church, South Newington

Photo: Brian Curtis

The church is one of only fifteen dedicated to St Peter ad Vincula ("St Peter in Chains").

Wall paintings were added to the north aisle around 1330–40. These include the Martyrdom of St Thomas a Becket, Virgin Mary with infant Jesus, and St Margaret the Virgin.

Angela Fortnum

Church Interior

Photo: Brian Curtis

Chapter 7

Joseph Page: Two-Times-GGF

Joseph was born in South Newington and baptised on 8 January 1815 at the parish church:

1815 PAGE Joseph s. John and Hannah weaver.

The marriage of Joseph and Harriet Timms took place at St Michael's Church, Great Barford—now Barford St Michael.

CERTIFIED COPY OF AN ENTRY OF MARRIAGE   GIVEN AT THE GENERAL REGISTER OFFICE

Application Number 6468697/2

18.. Marriage solemnized ....in the *Church* of *Great Bourton* in the County of *Oxford*.

No.	When Married	Name and Surname	Age	Condition	Rank or Profession	Residence at the Time of Marriage	Father's Name and Surname	Rank or Profession of Father
2	*February 7*	*Joseph Cage*	26	*Bachelor*	*Labourer*	*Williamscot*	*John Cage*	*Labourer*
		Harriet Timms	20	*Spinster*		*Bourton Mandville or Great Bourton*	*James Timms*	*Labourer*

Married in the *Church of Great Bourton* according to the Rites and Ceremonies of the *Church of England* by me,

This Marriage was solemnized between us,
The *Sign of Joseph Cage*
The *Sign of Harriet Timms*

in the Presence of us,
Thomas Cage
Eliza Wriggles

CERTIFIED to be a true copy of an entry in the certified copy of a register of Marriages in the Registration District of Banbury

Given at the GENERAL REGISTER OFFICE, under the Seal of the said Office, the   19th   day of   May   2015

MXG 535885

The marriage banns were called on the three proceeding Sundays at South Newington.

<u>1839</u> PAGE Joseph bach otp 27 Jan 3 and 10 Feb

TIMS Harriet spin of Great Barford

Due to illiteracy, the name Timms is spelled Tims and, in some instances, Timbs, hence, the difference between the marriage certificate and parish register.

Even though Joseph's father was parish clerk and therefore had a degree of literacy, Joseph was unable to sign his name. My explanation is that he was probably left-handed, which meant the ink used in those days would smudge. Left-handedness runs in the family, including me, but pens and inks have improved over the years.

1841 Census for South Newington

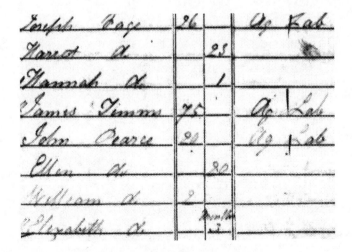

Seventy-five-year-old James Timms is Harriet's father.

Joseph and Harriet had four sons, and each had Tims as a forename:

James John Tims Page, Charles Tims Page (my GGF), Samuel Tims Page, and John Tims Page.

They also had three surviving daughters, Hannah Maria, Mary Ann and Sarah.

Sadly, James died on 22 January 1844, one day after his baptism, from inflammation of the throat.

The South Newington parish register records his burial:

1844 Jan 25 James John Tims Page 6 wks.

Hannah Maria married a shoemaker and lived in the village of Bloxham. Her eldest daughter married and eventually emigrated to Canada with her family.

Mary Ann married a widowed baker from Wiltshire. Sarah also married a baker, and they possibly both met their future husbands through the baking trade. Son John was also a baker and used to go around the village of Bloxham with his baker's cart.

Both the 1841 and 1851 census returns gave Joseph's occupation as labourer, but by 1861, he was a baker living at the bakehouse.

Joseph was a Primitive Methodist, and by 1860, a congregation of seven was set up in South Newington, and two years later, the number had increased to fifteen. The Primitive Methodist Chapel, a small stone building, was opened in 1875 at the opposite end of the high street to the parish church. The trustees included Joseph Page, baker and local preacher. The building is now a private dwelling.

The 1891 census for South Newington has Joseph Leopold Page, grandson, living with Joseph and Harriet. Young Joseph was the son of Samuel Tims Page and his first wife, Ellen Lucy Frost, who probably died in childbirth. When Joseph died on 24 June 1899 from old age, Harriet moved in with her youngest daughter, Sarah, who was married to Thomas Franklin, a baker in Kidlington, effectively leaving Joseph homeless, and he became a boarder with George Roberts, a cattleman on a farm at Bloxham.

In 1903, Joseph married Marth Garlick at Wallingford, and he became a postal worker at Reading. He died on 11 January 1961 at Battle Hospital, Reading. He told his children he had no relatives, so it would seem his father, stepmother, and siblings had nothing to do with him.

Meantime, Harriet died of old age at her daughter's home and was buried at South Newington 8 December 1902.

Joseph's younger brother, Thomas, was a Wesleyan Methodist and, on the second of November 1882, purchased a piece of land which, on 28 May 1883, he conveyed (without charge) to the fifteen trustees of a proposed new chapel.

Methodist Chapel Wigginton

Photo: Brian Curtis

The village of Wigginton is basically a triangular shape around St Giles Church and has the River Swere on one side.

Chapter 8

Charles Tims Page: GGF

Charles was born at South Newington and his baptism was recorded in the parish register:

1845 February 15 PAGE Charles Tims s. Joseph and Harriet baker.

The 1861 census for South Newington records Charles's occupation as an agricultural labourer, but by 1871, he was working with his father as a baker.

Charles married Mary Freeman on 23 December 1871 at St Nicholas Parish Church, Tadmarton.

1871 PAGE Charles Tims FA bach baker South Newington s. Joseph

FREEMAN Mary FA spin. Tadmarton d James lab.

Wit: Ellen TIMS xJames FREEMAN

x denotes that James made his mark as he was unable to sign his name.

St Nicholas Church, Tadmarton, is a Grade I listed Norman building which was enlarged in the thirteenth century when the bell tower was added.

Tadmarton is made of two parts; Upper and Lower. The 2001 census recorded a population of 430, which had increased to 541 by 2011.

On 31 May 1944, a Vickers Wellington bomber aircraft was on a training flight over Tadmarton when the pilot turned to port (left), the wing collapsed, and the aircraft crashed. The aircraft burst into flames, and sadly, all seven crew members were killed.

The 1881 census for Milcombe: Charles and Mary are living at Milcombe (Water) Mill, with three children, Harry James (my GF), Emily, and Edith. His occupation was miller in corn. The mill was situated on the River Swere just outside South Newington. The only evidence that there was ever a building is a few pieces of rubble. Percival James was an addition to the family by the 1891 census, and the family had moved to South Newington Mill.

On the 14 April 1905, Charles and Mary's daughter Edith was killed due to a riding accident. Family story has it that she was catapulted off her horse by the branch of a tree.

1905 Apr 18 PAGE Edith Laura 27 South Newington

Announcement in the Banbury Guardian dated 20 April 1905, page 1.

April 14 at South Newington Mill, Edith Laura, youngest daughter of CHARLES T. and MARY PAGE, aged 27 years.

Both Harry and Percival were married by the time of the 1911 census, and Charles and Mary were living with Percy and his wife, Alice.

My mother often told the story of how her grandfather, in his later years, would ring a bell, even if all he wanted was his tea stirred, and Percy's young children would go running to see what he wanted.

Percival and Alice had eight children: three boys and five girls. None of the boys married or had children, so the Page name did not continue through the male line. Herbert Charles (Bert) was the last son to die in 1999.

Charles died from a cerebral haemorrhage on 3 May 1931 at Holywell Farm, Wigginton, Oxfordshire.

Chapter 9

Harry James Page: GF

Harry was the eldest of four children born to Charles Tims Page and his wife, Mary. He was born at Milcombe Mill on 5 April 1873 and was baptised at St Laurence Church Milcombe:

<u>1873</u> Oct 5 PAGE Harry James s. Charles and Mary Milcombe Mill miller

St Laurence Church is small compared to those in surrounding villages but, nevertheless, is a well-proportioned building, made of local Horton stone. From 1854–1920s, Milcombe was a parish before being united with the neighbouring village of Bloxham. The nave was reroofed in the fifteenth century, and in subsequent years, it was necessary to undertake further repairs due to the building becoming derelict. An organ was installed in 1906 and was moved to its current location some forty years later.

Harry married Elizabeth Humphrey at St Mary's Church Islington on 5 October 1909. Harry was aged thirty-six and a miller and farmer of the mill, South Newington,

Elizabeth aged twenty-four, no occupation. Marriage banns were called at both St Mary's and South Newington:

1909 Harry James Page bch of St Peter ad Vincula South Newington Oxford

Elizabeth Humphrey spin of this parish 19 and 26 Sept and 3 Oct

1909 PAGE Harry James bch otp

HUMPHREY Elizabeth spin. Psh St Mary Islington Co Mddx 19 and 26 Sep and 3 Oct

Harry and Elizabeth had six children: two boys, one who died as a young child (from acute cerebral meningitis and convulsions), the other still living; and four girls, Winifred (Winnie), Muriel (my mother), Marjorie, and Kathleen.

1916 Feb 28 PAGE Harry Humphrey Claude 2 yrs SN

The name lives on through my uncle.

Winnie worked in a post office and married a widower, Henry (Bob), a retired London policeman. Marjorie married a local farmer and Kathleen a schoolmaster from Lancashire. I will say more about Muriel in the next chapter.

There is a family story about Kathleen, who was walking with a jug of milk and not paying attention to what she was doing when suddenly there was milk running all over the road!

The three younger girls were close together in age and were always getting into trouble like falling in the brook but, it was always harmless fun.

Mills of South Newington

"In 1086 there were two mills, valued at 4s. 2d. and 2s. 8d. a year. (fn. 243) Only one may be traced later, belonging to the Cranford manor and on the site of the surviving mill house north of the village. It was valued at 3s. 4d. in 1302, was empty and ruinous in 1357, but in 1368 was leased to a Bloxham miller. (fn. 244) In the 17th century the mill was owned by the King family; it was both a corn and fulling mill by 1712, and probably by 1624 when John King was a fuller. (fn. 245) There may have been other water mills in the parish, for in 1694 another John King devised to his grandson John French the mills next to his South Newington house and all his other mills in the parish. (fn. 246) The mill of William Green, miller (d. 1600), has not been identified. (fn. 247) Thomas French sold the South Newington mills to Thomas Barrett in 1712, and they passed thereafter to Henry Fowler of Shutford in 1729, Alexander Tredwell of Shenington (partly in 1736, wholly by 1759), William Tredwell (1759), Richard Faulkner of Broughton (1764), and William Robinson (by 1816). (fn. 248) By then the mill was used only as a corn mill. Robinson sold it to Richard Hall in 1845, but his family seem to have been working the mill in 1853. (fn. 249) From the 1880s to the late 1920s the mill was held by members of the Page family. (fn. 250) It was then acquired by D. P. Lithgow of the Manor House, who used it for private purposes until the Second World War. (fn. 251) The mill house survives but the watercourse has been diverted." From: 'Parishes: South Newington', A History of the County of Oxford: Volume 11: Wootton Hundred (northern part) (1983), pp. 143-159.

During the late 1920s, the family left the mill and moved to Ivy Dean in the high street. The property had a dining room, kitchen with family table, sideboard, and range, and wash house together with a toilet at the top of the garden.

The stairs to the second floor were winding, which as a young child I did not like. I must have gone upstairs, but my memory fails me as to what rooms were there.

There was a small garden and dairy, and outside the boundary wall, my grandmother kept chickens. There was a small orchard and the milking parlour.

In 1959, there was a small straw fire in the yard, and the fire brigade was called. One of the firefighters died at the scene, but the cause of death was recorded as "natural causes."

Harry passed away in the Horton General Hospital on 15 June 1959; the cause of death was congestive cardiac failure. I vividly remember the day we received a telegram from my uncle. Grandfather was buried at South Newington. Probate was granted to his widow at Oxford on 30 June.

Held in private family collection

Elizabeth died on 11 December 1961. She had been in the Churchill Hospital for treatment on her thyroid gland and was being taken home by daughters Kathleen and Muriel when she collapsed on the doorstep. She died in the Horton General Hospital. The coroner's verdict after a post-mortem but no inquest was

"Massive Pulmonary embolism. Venus thrombosis of the left leg. Carcinoma of the Thyroid Gland."

The land was subsequently sold off for housing development, and the house sold separately and extensively renovated.

Held in private family collection

Chapter 10

Postscript

Muriel Page and Angela Fortnum

The last two generations of my bloodline.

My mother was born on 28 December 1916. A day when there was a terrific amount of snow about, and my grandfather had to take the horse and cart to the next village to collect the nurse. He survived the trip and lived to tell the tale.

As previously mentioned, Mum lived at South Newington Mill and played with her siblings. As soon as she was old enough to find employment, she had several positions as a companion/housekeeper. I remember visiting two elderly spinsters in King's Sutton, a Northamptonshire village about five miles from Banbury. These elderly ladies gave me a silver spoon for my christening with a note saying:

"With love from N & E Milner to dear little Angela"

Muriel Page, aged twenty-one years

Held in private family collection

During the war years, my mother met my father, John Fortnum, and they married at St Mary's Parish Church, Banbury, on 3 September 1945. Food rationing was in operation; friends gave ingredients, so they could have a wedding cake. Dad worked on the railway and was exempt from action during the war, but he volunteered to join the Royal Engineers, his father's old regiment.

Banbury is an historic market town on the River Cherwell in Oxfordshire. The town's name comes from *Banna*, a Saxon chieftain, and *burgh*, meaning "settlement." The Domesday Book refers to it as "Banesberie", and in medieval times another spelling was "Banesbury".

For visits to the local villages, Banbury is a good base and is also not far from Shakespeare country.

Parish Church of St Mary Banbury

Photo: Angela Fortnum

John Fortnum in uniform

Held in private family collection

St Mary's Church was built in 1790 to replace the existing medieval church damaged during the English Civil War. It is a Grade I listed building with the tomb of Gulliver in the churchyard. Jonathan Swift is said to have seen the name and chose it for *Gulliver's Travels*. In the 1860s and 1870s, the vicar, Henry Back, an Anglo-Catholic, commissioned Arthur Bloomfield to decorate the church in a Byzantine style.

The resurrection chapel has eighty-four lamps of brotherhood, made after World War II as a sign of reconciliation.

David Thompson, vicar from 1984–94 became bishop of Huntingdon, and Anthony Williams, vicar from 1931–46, later became bishop of Bermuda.

Initially, Mum and Dad rented a flat before moving into a new home a few weeks before I was born in 1948. I live in this house today. I was baptised at Christchurch South in Banbury on 26 February 1949 having recovered from pneumonia.

<u>1949</u> Feb 26 FORTNUM Angela Mary d. John Wilfred George and Muriel Elizabeth *(address withheld)* Guard (Railway). Godparents Marjorie Rose Page, Kathleen Mildred Page and J.W.G. Fortnum.

The congregation reduced over time, and the building was demolished to be replaced by social housing.

I started school in 1953 and left to start my first and only job in banking in 1965. When I was eleven, Mum found herself a job, first in a shop and then in the offices of a factory.

Both parents were interested in the garden, Mum flowers and Dad vegetables, and used to show at the local flower and vegetable show winning many prizes.

Muriel and Angela with the Front Garden in the Background Circa 1967

Held in private family collection

I was the first to learn to drive, in 1967, followed by Mum and then Dad. The purchase of a car gave us more freedom with regards to visiting relatives and going on holiday.

In 1981, I was offered a position in the mortgage department in Birmingham, so when the job became permanent, on 1 April 1982, I went house hunting in the Shirley/Solihull area. This is the south side of Birmingham, which made it easier to get back to Banbury in case of need. I took early retirement in 1998, selling my house and returning to the family home.

Dad had already had a stroke and was being cared for by my mother, so it was good that I was also on hand to help with some of the running about. He passed away in a nursing home on 11 December 2001, aged ninety years, and was cremated at Banbury Crematorium on 17 December. His ashes were later interred and marked by a stone.

Mum was very good for her age but became frail during her mid-nineties and died in the Horton General Hospital on 16 August 2014, aged ninety-seven years, and was cremated on her wedding anniversary the 3 September 2014. Her ashes were interred with those of my father on 8 September.

Banbury Crematorium

I had more spare time and decided to research my bloodline and then their siblings. This led me to expand my research from genealogy to include family and religious history, with a view to possible publication.

I am looking forward to writing about another branch of my family.

Abbreviations

bach	bachelor
botp	both of this parish
d	daughter
GF	grandfather
GGF	great-grandfather
fa	full age
lab	labourer
otp	of this parish
psh	parish
s	son
SN	South Newington
spin	spinster
wit	witnesses

Bibliography

Ancestry.com 1841. England Census [database online] Provo, UT, USA. [accessed 2018.]

Ancestry.com 1851. England Census [database online] Provo, UT, USA. [accessed 2018.]

Ashbridge, Dr Pauline, *Village Chapels* (Kershaw Publishing, 2004). pp.77–8 and 84.

Baggs, A. P., Colvin, Christina, Colvin, H. M., Cooper, Janet, Day, C. J. Selwyn, Nesta and Tomkinson, A., *A History of the County of Oxford: Volume 11: Wootton Hundred (Northern Part)* (London, 1983).

Banburystmary.org.uk/ [accessed May 2018].

Britishlistedbuildings.co.uk/England/barford-st-john-and-barford-st-michael-cherwell-oxfordshire. [accessed May 2018].

Curtis, Brian. *Briancurtis@oxfordshirechurches.info*

Findmypast.co.uk Hertfordshire baptisms and burials transcripts 1670 [accessed August 2018].

Mann, Ralph, *Wigginton Methodist Chapel 1883–2008 125 Years.* (Wigginton Methodist Church, 2008).

Oxfordshire Family History Society. (2010) *OXF-BAN01 3rd Edition CD.* Banbury St. Mary parish register and Banbury South, Christchurch parish register. Oxfordshire Parish Registers Transcripts BANBURY Registration District Vol. 1.

Oxfordshire Family History Society. (2013) *OXF-BAN02 3rd Edition CD.* Bloxham parish register. Oxfordshire Parish Registers Transcripts BANBURY Registration District Vol. 2.

Oxfordshire Family History Society. (2013) *OXF-BAN04 3rd Edition CD.* Barford St Michael, Milcombe and South Newington parish registers. Oxfordshire Parish Registers Transcripts BANBURY Registration District Vol. 4.

Oxfordshirevillages.co.uk/cherwellvillages/the–barfords [accessed May 2018].

Surnamedb.com/surname/ [accessed April 2018].

Wikipedia.org/wiki/banbury. [accessed May 2018].

Wikipedia.org/wiki/bloxham [accessed May 2018].

Wikipedia.org/wiki/Plush. [accessed Apr 2018].

Wikipedia.org/wiki/south_newington [accessed April 2018].

Wikipedia.org/wiki/tadmarton [accessed May 2018]

Index

Paige:

           Elizabeth 4, 5, 8, 15, 21, 37, 38, 41, 47

           Mary x2 4, 5, 7, 8, 9, 15, 20

Pargeter,   Sarah 17

Roberts,   George 30, 47

Rymell:

           Dorathy 3, 4, 7

           John 4, 5, 6

Timms,   Harriet 27

Tunks,   Jane Elizabeth 15

White,   Mary 7

Towns and Villages:

           Banbury 34, 43, 44, 45, 47, 48, 49

           Barford St Michael and Barford St John 19, 20, 27

           Bloxham 15, 17, 18, 20, 29, 30, 37, 39

           South Newington 4, 7, 9, 14, 17, 20, 21, 22, 23, 24, 27, 28, 29, 30, 33, 34, 37, 38, 39, 40, 43

           Tadmarton 33, 34

           Wigginton 9, 31, 35,